FANTASTIC
Fun Face Painting

FANTASTIC
Fun Face Painting

Sherrill Leathem

Sterling Publishing Co., Inc.
New York

Library of Congress
Cataloging-in-Publication Data Available

2 4 6 8 10 9 7 5 3 1

Published in 1997 by Sterling Publishing Company, Inc.
387 Park Avenue South, New York, N.Y. 10016

Originally published in Great Britain in 1996 by Ebury Press
as *The Complete Book of Face Painting*
Text © 1996 Sherrill Leathem
Photography © 1996 Ebury Press

Distributed in Canada by Sterling Publishing
c/o Canadian Manda Group, One Atlantic Avenue, Suite 105
Toronto, Ontario, Canada M6K 3E7

Printed and bound in Portugal

Sterling ISBN 0-8069-9850-4

CONTENTS

INTRODUCTION

Turn a boy into a lion and he will find it hard not to let out a mighty roar. With the face of a queen to hide behind, even a shy girl will take on a new personality. Give adults a mask and they too can relive their childhood, becoming their favorite movie star, or the clown they once saw at the circus.

By entering the creative world of face painting, you can ignore reality and make beasts out of beauties, transform school kids into superheroes and age the young before they get old.

All ages like to role-play and fantasize and, with the help of MIMICKS FACE PAINTING, you can create a cast of new characters to fulfill your wildest dreams.

GETTING STARTED

Take a good look at your own face in the mirror and discover how it works. Feel the bone structure and the contrasting fleshy areas. Even without face paint, you can imagine the scowl of a dreadful monster or the coy smile of a demure princess. Try grinning like a crazy clown or growling like a tiger and then see what happens to your eyes, eyebrows, mouth and chin. You can use face paints to emphasize your features in lots of wonderful ways to create hundreds of truly different expressions.

Face painting has never been so much fun. With this book, a set of face paints, sponges and a few brushes, you will soon have all the techniques and ideas you need to create fantastic faces.

> **IMPORTANT**
> Before starting, check that the person you are painting does not have a skin allergy, eye infection or cold sore. Never use face paints under such circumstances.

PRODUCTS

The best face paints to use are water based because they are easy to apply and give a professional result. By mixing the basic colors together in a lid or on a plate, you can make new shades. Once dry, these paints give a matte appearance and rarely rub off unless they get wet. To remove water-based paints, simply wash off with soap and water. Use a mild cleansing cream to remove paint around and under the eyes.

Use good-quality brushes, such as sable brushes, because they are easy to control and maintain their flexibility. You will need an assortment of brushes to paint different strokes. You'll use flat-edged bristles for blending and creating large areas of color, and rounded and pointed bristles for making fine lines and adding intricate details.

Use synthetic or natural sponges to apply a base layer of color. Fine or coarse stipple sponges are good for creating special effects such as bruising, stubble, or for softening areas of paint.

To add instant sparkle to your work, apply a quick-drying glitter gel — available in a variety of colors.

Check that you have the following basic items before you start:

Table and chair

Water-based face paints

Old towel or cloth — to place your paints on

Sponges — one for each different color

Brushes — assorted shapes and sizes

Water in a bowl or dish — plus access to a fresh supply of water

Lid or plate — for mixing colors

Baby wipes — to clean dirty faces

Smock or towel — to protect clothing

Gray makeup pencil — for outlining

Mirror — perhaps most important of all

For more adventurous designs you will also need:

Glitter gel — to add sparkle

Stipple sponges — fine and coarse

Colored makeup powders

Powder brushes

You can purchase the products below from most good toy stores, and from art and theatrical shops.

THE BASIC TECHNIQUE

Place all your equipment, including the paints, within easy reach of the hand you are using to paint. Protect clothing by placing a smock or towel around the child's shoulders and, if necessary, push the hair back with a hair band.

Begin by cleansing the face with a baby wipe. Next apply a base layer of paint using a damp sponge (see opposite). You can add other colors to the base to create different face tones, either by creating blocks of color or by blending colors for a softer effect. Use one sponge per color and, after use, wash each thoroughly in a bowl of mild soapy water.

When the base is dry, you may find it helpful to outline your design first with a soft gray makeup pencil. To fill in the details of your design, you should hold your brush like a pencil, resting your little finger comfortably somewhere on the face. This will provide balance to your hand. Paint in the lightest colors first and, where possible, start at the forehead and work down.

Face painting is easier when the child sits on a sturdy table, as shown here. This is the best position because it is possible to move around to paint each side of the face without twisting the child's head to and fro.

Take great care when outlining the delicate eye area, especially if the child is finding it hard to sit still.

With a little practice, you will soon be able to apply an even base in no time at all, leaving you free to experiment. As your painting skills progress, try creating your own designs.

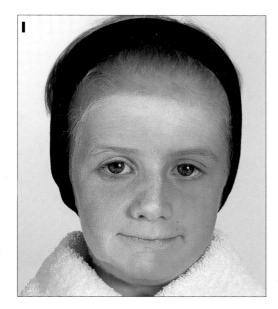

1 Take a damp, but not wet, sponge and stroke it over the paint a couple of times to build up a layer. Test its consistency on the back of your hand because it should not be too wet or the paint will streak. Start at the forehead and work downwards in quick sweeping movements. Pay attention to the creases around the eyes, nose and mouth.

2 When you are satisfied with your base, you may wish to add a second border tone. Blend the edges together with soft dabbing strokes. If the base starts to streak or bubble, then your sponge is too wet. Simply squeeze out the excess water and reapply the paint.

3 For a more colorful face, add a third border tone and repeat the soft dabbing strokes. The paint dries quickly, so you need to be fast when blending to ensure good coverage. Check that all the edges around the jawline are solid and even. If you wish to create a face using different colors, you will find it is easier to start at the chin.

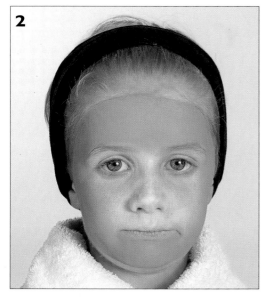

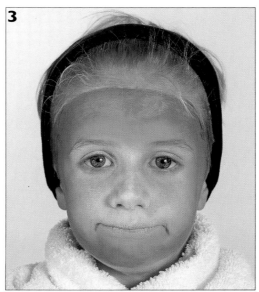

Animals made popular by cartoons, such as mice and bunnies, are quite easy to face-paint. Look closely at animal pictures to find a facial feature that you can exaggerate. To create these faces, the teeth of both the field mouse and the rabbit were over-emphasized. Notice how both sets of teeth start from different points – the mouse's teeth are painted from the nose down and the rabbit's from the bottom lip. Adapt the following instructions for the Field Mouse to create the Bunny Rabbit.

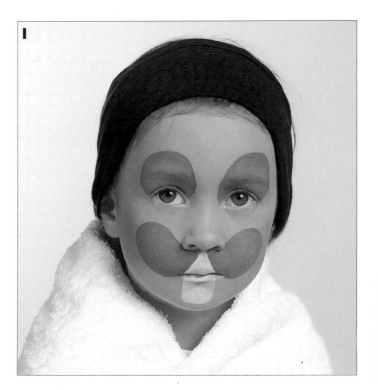

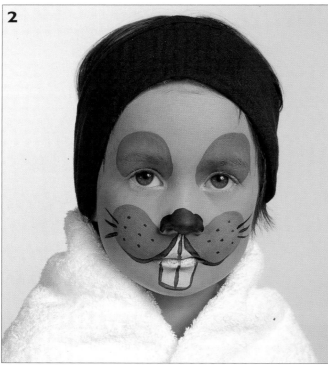

1 Sponge on a skin-colored base and cover the cheek-bones with pink powder. Using a wide brush, paint a tapered white stripe from the nose down through the mouth and chin. Paint big circles around the eyes in light brown. Add two high curved shapes in the same color for the cheeks.

2 Use black to outline the edge of the lower cheek from under the nose, sweeping up and out along the curve to a point. Still using black, add the whiskers and dots. Carefully outline the large teeth.

Let your imagination run wild when painting feline faces. Not only can you paint them in their actual browns, oranges and reds, but you can also use blues, pinks and greens to create comical cats. The simplest cat or dog only needs a basic black nose and whiskers. For a more elaborate effect, add a fluffy muzzle and incorporate some furlike markings. Notice how tying the young girl's hair into bunches has given the Playful Pup some instant droopy ears.

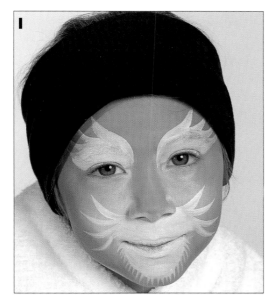

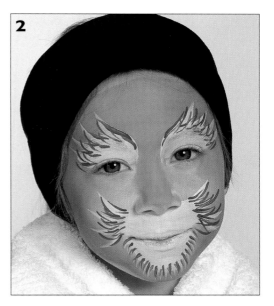

1 Sponge on a full white base and add an orange border tone around the edges and down the nose. Lightly blend in a third tone of red. Paint in the white eye shapes by starting at the inner corners and sweeping the brush up and out to a point. Repeat using similar strokes for the muzzle.

2 Add flecks of red and brown to the outer edges of the white pattern around the eye and muzzle areas to give a fluffy appearance.

3 Now paint some brown wavy fur markings on the forehead and the cheeks. Using black paint, block in the eyelids and the end of the nose. From under the nose, divide the muzzle in two with a wide smile. Color the bottom lip black and finish with some dots for whiskers.

TIGER

The striking markings of the big cats lend themselves really well to face paints. Because tigers, leopards and lions all share basic characteristics, you can use the same procedure for the base, eye and muzzle before adding their distinctive fur markings. Paint wavy forked lines on the face for a tiger. Use groups of square dots to suggest a leopard's coat. Use long feathery strokes to indicate a lion's shaggy mane.

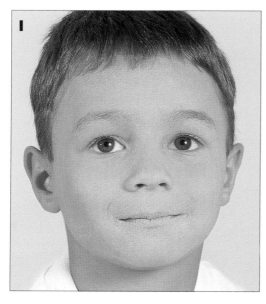

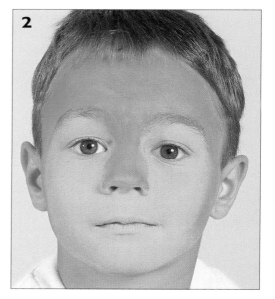

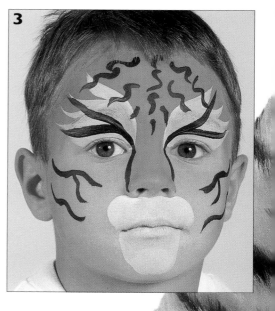

FABULOUS FAKE FUR
Fake fur is inexpensive and widely available, so why not complete the look with a "big cat" suit. Make the head in a simple hood-shape, adding two rounded ears.

1 Sponge on a yellow base to cover the whole face.

2 Add a border tone of orange to cover the forehead, the nose and the sides of the face.

3 Paint in white zigzag shapes sweeping up from each eye. Create a solid area of white for the muzzle. Sweep two black forked lines up and outward from each eye. Extend these lines down the sides of the nose. Add black squiggles to the forehead and cheeks to indicate fur markings. To finish, dip a flat-edged brush in black paint, hold it under the nose and flick it upwards to give a furry look. Paint a black line down from the nose and across the upper lip, and add some dots for whiskers.

BIRD OF PARADISE

You can paint this beautiful bird of paradise in a range of different colors. Try using pastel shades of pink, mint and yellow for a soft, subtle look. For a striking, dramatic effect, sponge on a three-color base in purple, blue and green, and then complete with a range of black, gold or silver feathery markings. When using glitter on any face, be careful not to place it too close to the eyes.

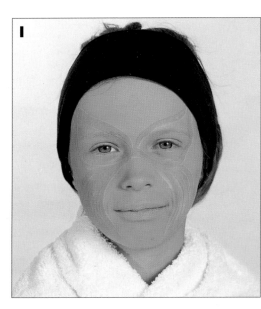

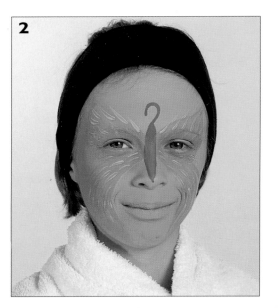

FANCY FEATHERS
Create a fantasy costume to complement your painted face by simply tying a colorful feather boa around your shoulders and adding a feather or two to your hair.

1 Sponge on a skin-colored base. Using a pale blue, paint the outline of the wings, starting at the nose and sweeping up and out to a point. Then curve this line down under the eyes, before extending long spiky strokes downwards to indicate the outer edges of the lower wings.

2 Using a wide brush, color the wings in pale blue. Paint a dark blue bird's body down the middle of the nose, adding a hooked head shape in the middle of the forehead. Using yellow paint, dab fine feathery brush strokes at random all over the wings.

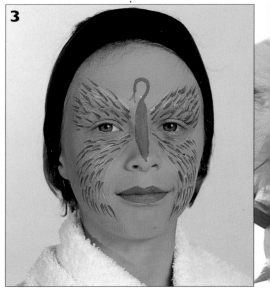

3 Add more feather marks to the wings in red and dark blue. Place a small red beak and white eye dot on the head of the bird. Finally, paint the child's mouth red and sprinkle the face with lots of glitter.

CREEPY CRAWLY

This creepy face is enough to make anyone's legs start to wobble. By taking a closer look at the creepy crawly world around you, you'll find all sorts of horrors to draw inspiration from. Try painting that daddy longlegs that climbs up the wall, or maybe just a simple bug on the end of a nose. Don't forget you can always include other small details such as a web or honey pot, to make it that little bit more realistic!

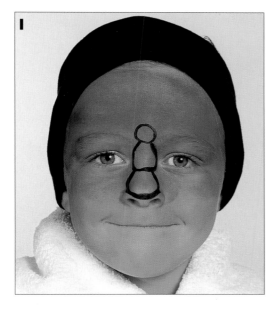

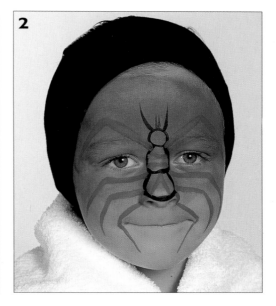

1 Starting at the chin and working upwards, sponge on a base in purple, green and yellow. Be sure to blend all the edges of the colors together. Paint three circles in black down the nose to form the spider's body.

2 Change to orange and paint some markings across the spider's body. Add the eight legs – one pair above the eyebrows and the other three pairs slanting out from the nose. Add the antennae in black.

3 To make the legs hairy, simply paint small black lines across and down the length of each leg. Finally, color the body shape in black.

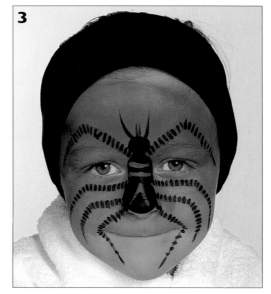

BUTTERFLY

When this brightly painted butterfly shows its face, it's obvious that spring cannot be far away! With all sorts of possible color combinations, you can match the color of the butterfly to the child's clothing as a final touch. As an alternative to the design shown here, try painting butterfly motifs on the cheeks or over one eye, perhaps including a garland of flowers.

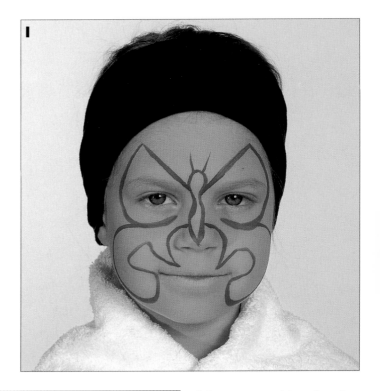

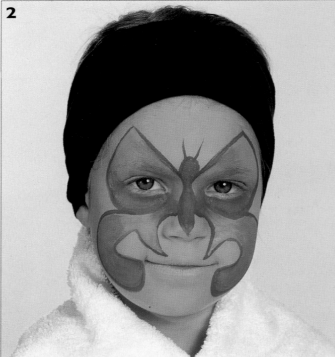

1 Sponge on a skin-colored base. Using a fine brush, outline the butterfly's body, wings and antennae in dark blue. Check that each side of the face is symmetrical.

2 Fill in the butterfly with three complementary colors (purple, bright pink and pale blue were used here). Using a slightly damp brush, blend the colors evenly together.

3 Paint some dark blue scallop-shape markings all over the wings. Scatter some glitter all over the design. You may also decide to paint the mouth.

The graceful swan, with its elegant simplicity, is another creature that lends itself very well to face painting. Rather than a black swan on a light background, try painting white swans on a dark blue base. Add your own style of floral decoration or perhaps just a few simple swaying grasses. For a romantic touch, paint two swans facing each other over the eyes, where they will seem to be kissing.

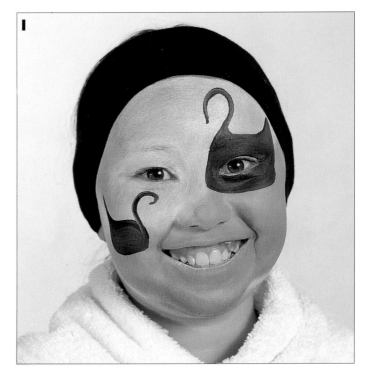

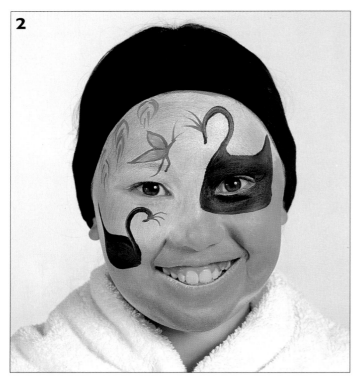

1 Sponge on a full white base. Blend in some green around the chin area. Add pale blue and blend this shade lightly up to one eye. Using a wide brush, paint an oval shape for each swan, bringing the tail end to a point. Add the hooked head and neck.

2 With a fine brush, paint the swan's head crown in dark blue. Outline a butterfly in dark blue on the forehead, adding multicolored wings and random sprays of color as decorative touches.

3 Adorn the lake with orange and green reeds. Add white feather marks to the swans and ripples to the lake. Paint tiny red beaks on the swans and give the child a prominent red mouth. Sprinkle some glitter over the final design.

CLOWNING AROUND

Because clowns come in all shapes and sizes and are famous for letting all their emotions show on their faces, you can have a lot of fun creating a clown. Circus clowns can be happy, sad, angry, pensive, wide-eyed – you name it, the list is endless. If you want to be a sad Pierrot Clown, experiment with a contrasting two-toned base instead of the traditional white makeup. The crazy Circus Clown will look good dressed in any clashing combination of colors. Clowns are ideal for people without much experience in face painting because they are easy to paint on small children. You can achieve the look with just a few basic details.

The instructions shown here are for a simple clown face that will appeal to all ages.

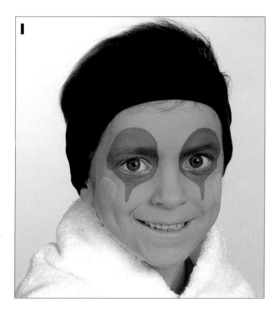

1 You can paint this face with or without a base. Start by painting high arches in green over the eyes. Sweep the color under the eyes, coming to a center point. Paint yellow circles on the cheeks.

2 Add a blue border line to the green area around the upper eye. Paint a greatly enlarged white mouth from the tip of the nose, over both the cheeks and chin. Using red, add a small circular nose. Finish by using the red to color the lips and outline the white mouth shape.

Toys can provide inspiration for countless different looks. These faces are based on the toys that young children love to play with. However, there's nothing to stop you from making the little boy look like a favorite rag doll and the girl like his army soldier. The camouflage army face is very easy to create and looks particularly effective beneath a matching army cap!

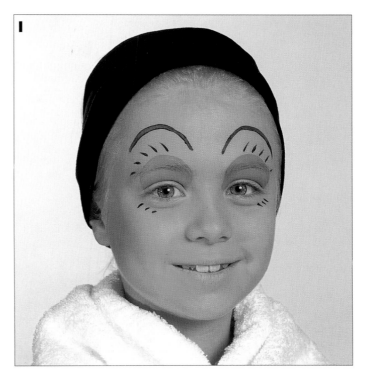

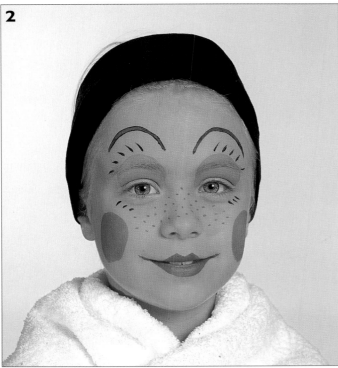

1 Sponge on a skin-colored base. Paint pale blue arches above the eyes. With a fine brush, paint black wispy eyelashes above and below the eyes. Still using black, paint thin curved eyebrows high up on the forehead.

2 Dab little dots of light brown across the nose to represent freckles. Paint in big round pink cheeks and apply some glitter. Paint the mouth a happy, upturned red. As you can see, the bright yellow wig is the crowning glory of this simple design.

Children of all ages love superheroes, and nothing will make you more popular than having the power to transform them into their latest hero. Simply by flipping through books, comics, magazines, and computer game manuals, you will find many faces which you can easily adapt. For a really dramatic touch, extend the color of the face into the hair by using either a toothbrush or spare sponge loaded with paint.

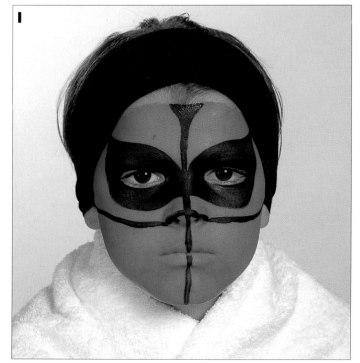

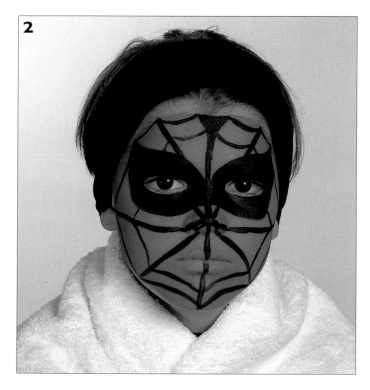

1 Sponge on a dense red base. Paint a pointed black mask around the eyes. Using a fine brush, start at the forehead and paint a vertical line through the face. Next, paint the horizontal line under the mask shape.

2 Continuing with the black paint, separate each quarter of the face again into halves. You will now have eight dividing lines. Lace the web together using a series of curved strokes.

3 Highlight the mask edge in white and place a black spider precariously somewhere within the web.

ICE FAIRY

Legend has it that some fairies can be found at the bottom of the garden under a toadstool, but others sparkle and shimmer in a much colder land. To enter the magical kingdom of the Ice Fairy, use cool blues, pink and white to represent snow and ice. For the fire fairy, use warm red with yellow and gold to represent flames. The garden fairy might work best in earthy oranges and browns.

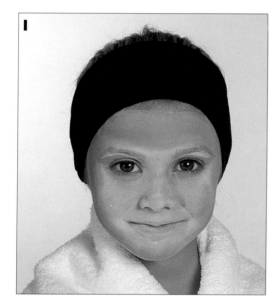

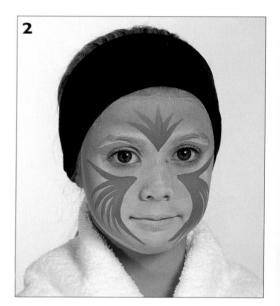

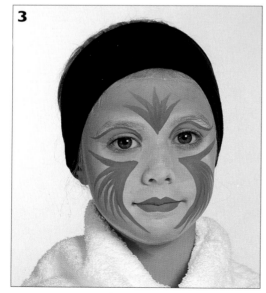

1 Sponge on a pale white base, and blend in a blue border tone. Paint a pale blue wing shape on each eyelid.

2 Dip the brush in bright blue and paint the spiky triangular shapes onto the forehead. Streak a line under the eyes, with a series of similar spiked strokes across the cheeks.

3 Change the color to bright pink and repeat smaller spiky strokes over the top of the bright blue spikes. Outline the eye shapes in pink. Add a blue mouth and decorate the design with dashes of glitter.

EVIL QUEEN

This simple, yet stunning, Evil Queen works well on both children and adults. The whole appearance hinges on the way the eyebrows are positioned. Look in the mirror and watch how your eyebrows change shape as your expression changes from modest to wicked. Adults could use soap to hide their natural eyebrow hair. Paint a thinner lip line for an even more sinister effect.

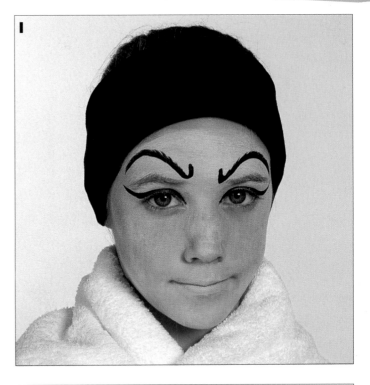

1 Sponge on a pale white base or alternatively a skin-colored one. Using black, paint in the eyelids, finishing with a dramatic curl. With a fine brush, sketch high arched eyebrow lines and lightly feather the top edges.

2 Paint in the area over the eye sockets in dark blue and add a paler blue up to the shaped eyebrows. Blend the two shades together using a slightly damp brush.

3 Using a blue sparkly powder or dry paint, brush over the cheeks and sides of the nose. Add some dark blue swirling "tentacles" to the cheeks, ending in a gold glitter dot. Finish with a cold blue mouth.

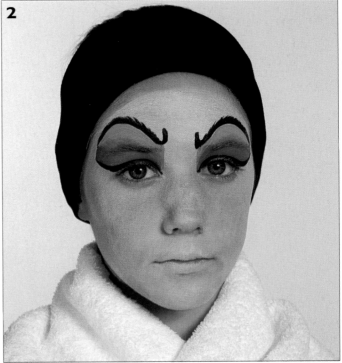

AYDREAMER

Creating a face based on a fantasy provides endless fun for your imagination. You can use any shape or form and any combination of colors, from bright and sharp to soft and hazy. Nothing needs to be symmetrical to achieve this look. Paint marks placed at random work as well as planned ones. Colored hair sprays that wash out help complete this otherworldly creation.

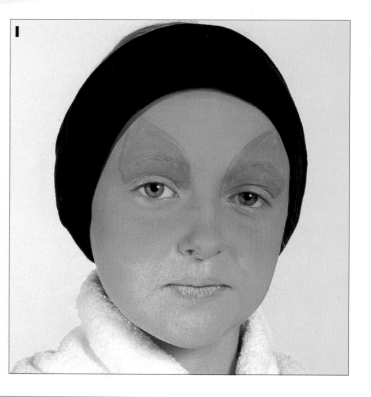

1 Sponge on a base in pink and yellow. Alternatively, try using mint and lilac. Paint pale blue pointed shapes around each eye.

2 Decorate the forehead and cheeks with dark blue stars and gold droplets. Add some sparkling glitter. Paint black wings curling upwards from each eyelid.

3 Using a fine brush, extend the eyeline down the sides of the nose and then streak it back up and outward. Add some lower lashes. Finally, paint the mouth red.

ELECTRIC SHOCKER

You can achieve startling effects with faces based on different kinds of weather. Electric Shocker reflects a deep, dark and menacing storm. When you add a red line of paint directly under the lower lashes, the eyes appear bloodshot and terrorized. You can achieve an altogether calmer look by painting golden sun rays on the base, or perhaps by painting a multicolored rainbow and a pot of gold.

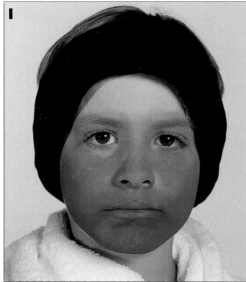

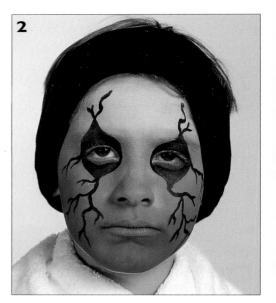

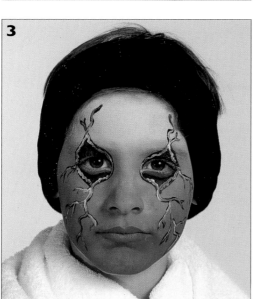

1 Sponge on a base in white, pale blue and dark blue. Blend all the edges together.

2 Paint a thin red line under the lower lashes. Change to black and paint the eye patches. Using a fine brush, paint single crooked lines coming out of the eye shapes, adding forked lines at random.

3 Create some lightning flashes by painting white through all the black lines and around the eye patches. Finish with a dramatic black or dark blue mouth.

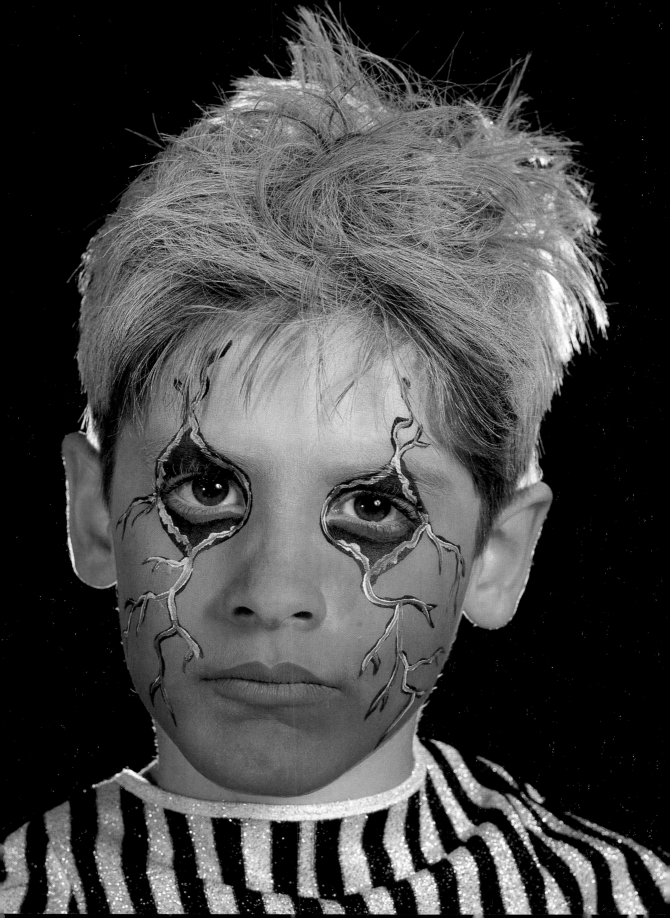

SWEETHEART

Because hearts are a symbol of romance, this face would be perfect for Valentine's Day. For a very small child you could paint a simple red heart on each cheek. Note the use of a skin-colored base, widely used throughout the book because it gives a natural complexion to work on and doesn't distract the eye from the painted design.

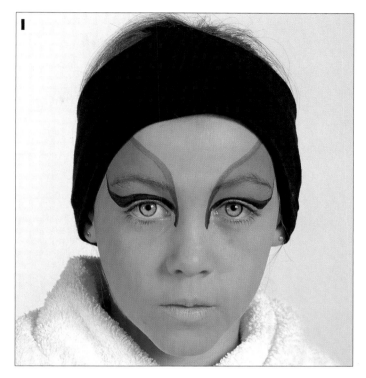

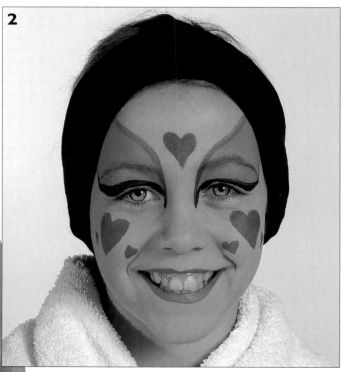

1 Sponge on a skin-colored base. Paint the black winged shapes above the eye, rising up and out to a point. Echo this shape in bright pink from the eyelids to either side of the forehead and outline the inner edges in red.

2 Paint hearts on the cheeks and forehead and add a scattering of red glitter. Paint the mouth red and then join the mouth to the cheeks with a sweep of gold glitter.

If you are interested in sports, you can paint many different faces to show your support. Try painting the colors of your favorite hockey, baseball or football team on your face. You could even add a team name or slogan to your design. You can show your support for a more individual sport, such as tennis, by painting a pair of miniature rackets on your cheeks. The sports shield on the face of this young football fan would also work well when painted on an arm as a tattoo.

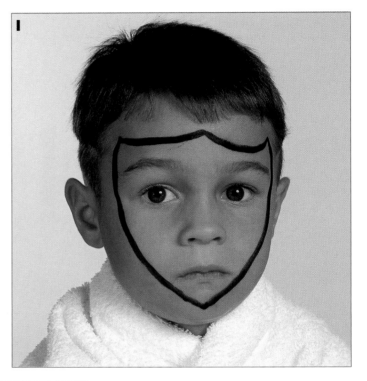

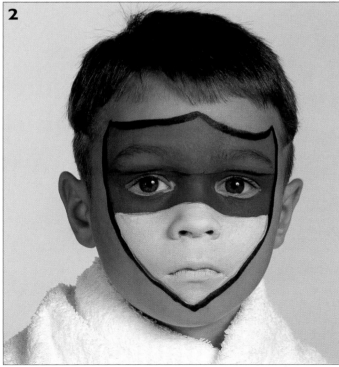

1 Starting at the forehead, outline the shape of the shield in black.

2 Divide the shield into three sections, painting the top part red, the middle blue and the bottom white.

3 Paint wide stripes in red and thinner stripes in blue throughout the white area.

The spiritual side of life can provide inspiration for face painting. This face draws upon astrology to portray a flaming sun depicting the twelve equal constellations of the zodiac. Using the sun, moon and stars, you can create endless different looks. The Yin Yang is based on the ancient Chinese philosophy of balance. This face has been painted in pinks and purples, unlike the traditional black and white version.

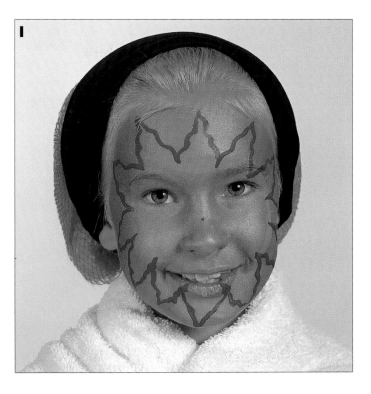

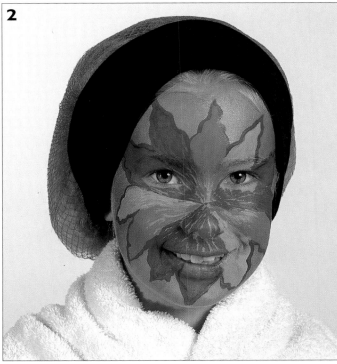

1 Sponge on a gold base. Paint a circle around the face close to the eyes and above the mouth in a skin tone color. Next divide this circle into twelve equal sections. With dark blue on a fine brush, use your dividing marks to outline the twelve wavy peaks. Place a central blue dot on the nose.

2 Starting at the forehead and rotating clockwise, paint the peaks alternately in blue, yellow, red and purple, lightly sketching each color towards the central dot. To finish, add a dark blue moon and stars to the design and sprinkle with glitter.

MASQUERADE

Mimick masks are ideal if you don't want children to paint details around their mouth. Be bold when painting masked faces. I find the darker and more prominent the colors, the more stunning the results. You can't go wrong in decorating your mask faces with a sprinkling of glitter or adhesive jewels. You can paint them with or without a base and experiment to create your own designs.

Monster

All small children seem to love being made up to look like four-legged monsters, such as reptiles and dinosaurs. You will be amazed to see your angelic child become a ghastly green, sharp-fanged imaginary beast! By painting distinctive features, like a row of painted teeth on the face, you quickly lose sight of the child and confront the most frightening and fiendish of faces.

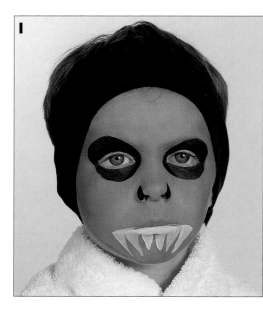

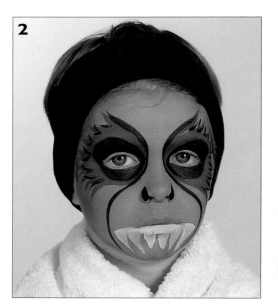

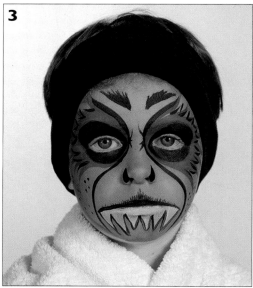

1 Sponge on a green base and stipple yellow down through the middle of the face. Using black, paint solid oval shapes around the eyes and along the edge of the nostrils. Change to white and paint a line along the bottom lip, extending it sideways in each direction. Paint some fangs downwards from this line, coming to a point at the chin.

2 Around the black eyes, paint spiky eye shapes in red. Feather the edges in black and sweep a wavy line down from the eyes to the outer fangs. This will help to bring the center of the face forward.

3 Still using black, paint a pair of hairy eyebrows and some frown lines between the eyes. Add an extended line of black to the top lip and use thin brush strokes to create the appearance of hair growth. Outline the fangs in black and add some dots to the cheeks.

We have all read fairy tales in which giant ogres were quite happy to make a meal out of human beings. Unspeakable monsters, they used to go about their business without so much as a thought for their victims. This interpretation presents a very different face of the ogre. Here, he is crooked, sullen and confused. Instead of showing a cruel monster, this face displays his softer side.

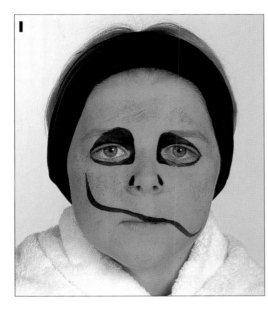

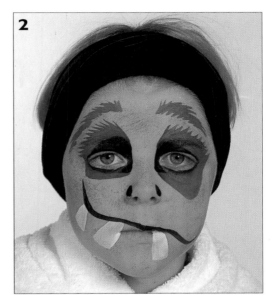

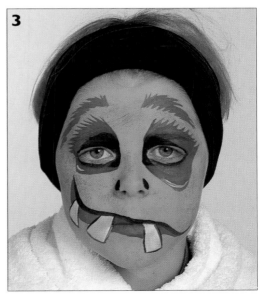

1 Sponge on a yellow base and roughly stipple with some orange blemishes. Give the eyes a soulful look by encircling them in black, squaring up the inner edges against the nose. Add black nostrils and a long lopsided line to represent the mouth.

2 Using a rust color, paint whiskery eyebrows high on the forehead and a shaggy uneven line around the eye shapes. Paint three broad white teeth protruding from the black mouth line.

3 Highlight the lower edge of the eye shapes with a white streak. Create a new mouth by filling in the lower lip line in red and outline the bold teeth in black. Finally, add some smudgy black stippling to the face.

Bones

You hope you won't bump into ghosts, ghouls and goblins in the night! Apart from the spooky appeal, children will love this idea for face painting. With a little extra work, you can easily transform the whole body into a skeleton perfect for fancy parties. Simply sketch out the basic bone structure on black paper and fill in the appropriate areas in white paint.

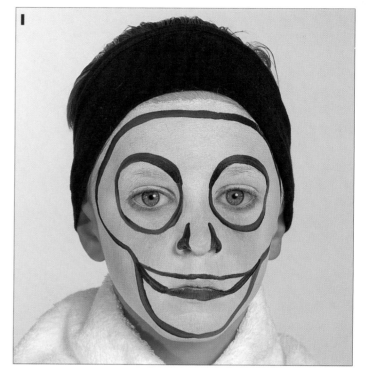

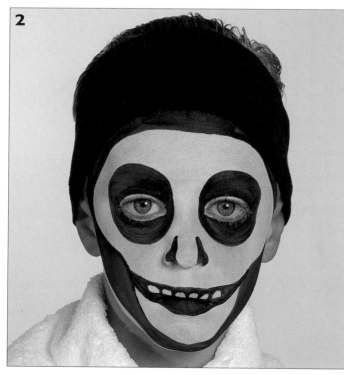

1 Sponge or paint a heavy white base. With black on a brush, outline the eye sockets and nostrils. Paint a skull shape around the edges of the face and draw an elongated mouth across the width of the skull.

2 Using black on a large brush, fill in the solid eye sockets and nostrils. Use black to paint around the outside of the skull shape. If necessary, build up the density with two coats. Add some bony teeth lines.

NIGHTSHADE AND WEREWOLF

The eerie world of the supernatural offers many possibilities for face painting. You will be surprised to discover that the simplest silhouettes and solid black shapes over a multicolored background can have a spellbinding effect. In addition, the dramatic use of strong black lines to exaggerate the eyebrows and create fangs on the Werewolf's face are easy to create. If you change the base for the Nightshade to a plain green one and add some warts, this face will indeed cast an evil eye.

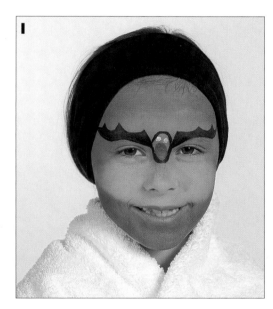

1 Sponge on a base in blue, pink, yellow and green. Using black on a brush, outline an oval shape to represent the bat's body on the bridge of the nose. From this, sweep a line up and out over the eyebrows, and scallop the top of the wings. Inside the oval, paint a red circle and two smaller white ones.

2 Paint some small black bats across the forehead. Color in the bat's head around the red and white circles and add the ears. From inside one eye, paint four lines downwards and join to form a web. Hang a black spider from the other eye.

3 Add tiny white fangs and small black pupils to the bat's face. Paint the child's mouth black and turn up one corner and turn down the other corner for a crooked effect. Dab the forehead with silver glitter.

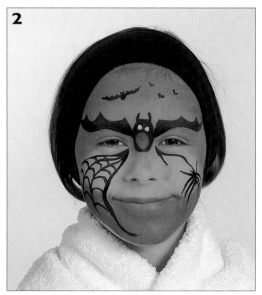

THE LIVING DEAD

To create this nightmare apparition, watercolors have been made to look like blood, because they are an easy, cheap and safe option for young children. Another possibility is to buy fake blood capsules, available from most good toy shops and theatrical suppliers. However, if you wish to simulate blood on older children or adults, you could track down "film blood," a fake blood product used for film and TV work. Try mixing a few coffee grounds with it to form lumpy blood clots. Beware of this product because it can irritate the eyes and stain clothing.

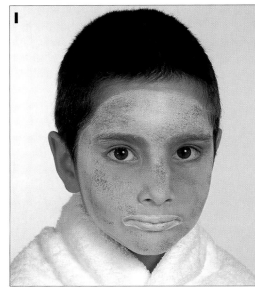

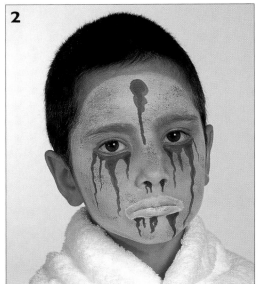

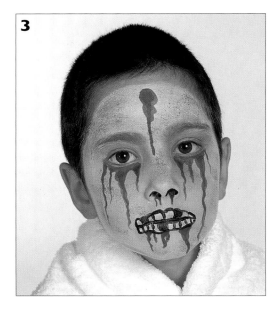

1 Sponge on a patchy white base and lightly stipple some areas with red. Brush on a dark gray powder or dry paint around the eye sockets. Paint a white oblong shape over the mouth and add a touch of yellow to it.

2 With red, paint a bullet hole on the forehead and a line under each eye. Paint some lines trickling down from the eyes, nostrils and mouth. You will then need to paint a darker red or brown on top of the flowing blood to give these depth.

3 Using a fine brush with black, outline the mouth and nostrils. Put in the teeth lines and color over a few to simulate gaps.

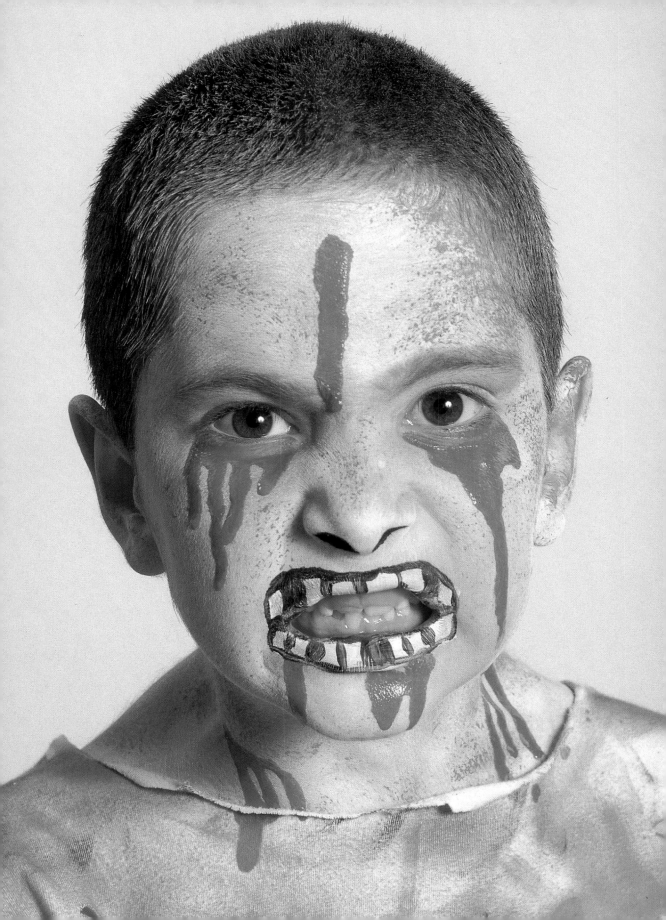

Hands and Feet

By using your imagination, you can coordinate most of the face designs in this book with matching hands and feet. The Evil Queen could have her fingers adorned with sparkling rings and colorful bracelets wrapped around her wrists, or you could continue the theme you have painted on the face, as shown here with the Tiger's Paw and the Skeleton Hand.

As when painting faces, it is sometimes best to first sponge a base over the area you wish to paint. Allow this to dry before adding your design.

TIGER'S PAW

1 Sponge an orange base over the hands and the lower half of the arms. Allow to dry.

2 Use black and white paints to imitate the tiger's forked, wavy markings, then make short, straight strokes over the fingers to give the impression of fur.

3 Finally, paint sharp black claws over the fingernails. You can adapt this design for other animals.

SKELETON HAND

1 Sponge a black base over the hands and the lower half of the arms. Allow to dry.

2 With white paint, make the bonelike shapes over the upper wrists and hands, and along each finger.

3 Finish by painting the fingernails white. When you have had some practice you can try painting your whole body!

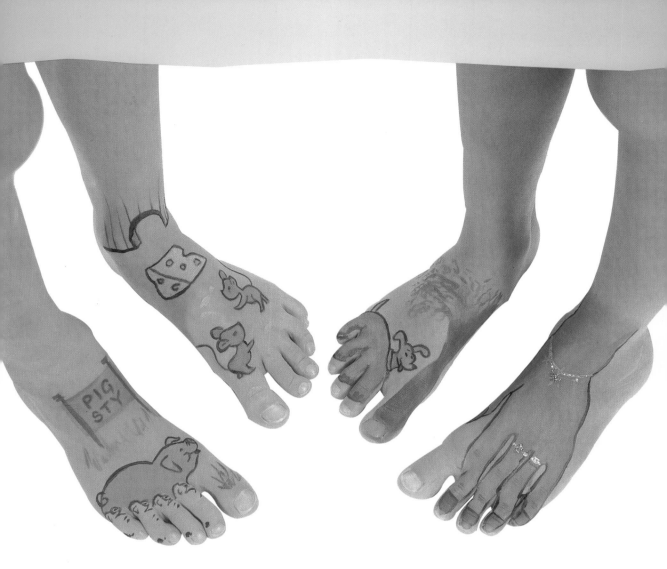

As well as coordinating your hands with your face, you can also paint your feet to match the designs on your face. You could give the Ogre green feet with black spiky claws and red veins, or paint some clown shoes with colorful bows and striped socks for the clown. Try painting footwear such as fluffy slippers or baseball boots on feet.

Alternatively, paint a quick amusing scene like the ones above. You and your friends can have lots of instant fun painting each other's feet with all sorts of designs.

TATTOOS

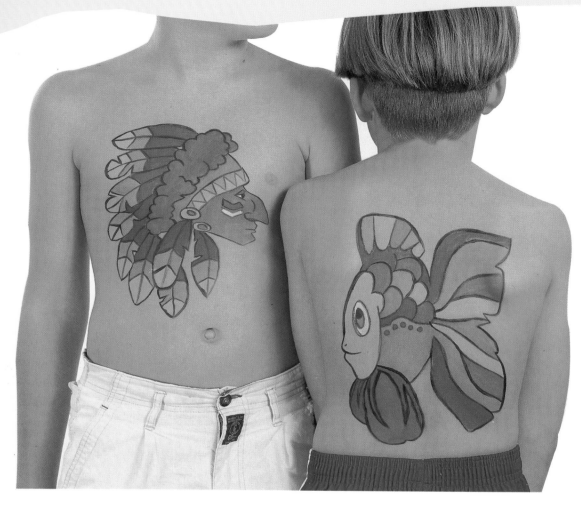

Do not be afraid to try your hand at these tattoos. You don't have to draw directly onto the skin until you've had a chance to work out your design on paper first. Big, bold designs with a strong black outline work best. These not only look good but are the easiest to paint. You can find inspiration in your children's favorite books, videos and TV programs.

1 Simply trace your artwork onto tracing paper using a soft pencil. With a wet cotton wool pad, dampen the area of skin and place your transfer on top (pencil side down).

2 Rub the back of the tracing paper with the cotton wool and then peel away to reveal a faint outline for guidance.

3 Using a black makeup pencil, go over the outline of your design – you are then ready to color in your tattoo.

THE AGING PROCESS

Making young people look old is much more fun and rewarding than watching our own faces age! We've used cream makeup for this sequence, although you can also use watercolor paint. Here the two children are 8 and 10. Dressed in the appropriate clothing, they look like senior citizens. This makeup is perfect for children playing adult roles in school and drama productions.

Applied quite crudely, this makeup works best at a distance. Use a more subtle effect for close-ups. Adapt the colors for dark skins and use a similar method to age the neck, hands and feet. You can apply skin-colored water-based paint to the hair on a toothbrush to give a natural graying appearance.

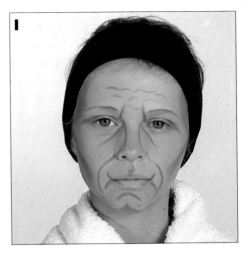

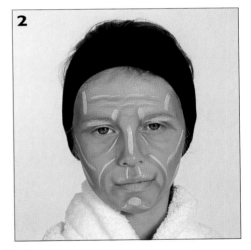

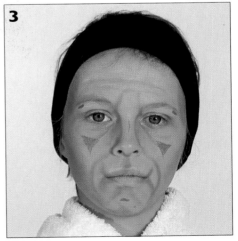

1 Apply a pale foundation thinly over the face with a latex sponge. Change to a medium brown color and shade the temples, cheekbones and jawline with your fingertips. Next use a fine brush to add lines to the forehead, eyebrows, eyes, area under the eyes, sides of the nose, nose hollow, smile lines, corners of the mouth and chin. With a clean, dry brush, blend in these shading lines.

2 Now using an ivory color on a brush, add highlights to the areas you have already shaded. With another clean, dry brush blend the highlights. If you are using cream makeup, set each stage of application with a loose translucent powder.

3 Apply a reddish brown color to the outer eyes, cheeks and chin by brush. Place a very pale line under the lower lashes and a dot on the end of the nose. Stipple the color with your fingertips. Finally, ask your model to pucker his or her mouth and sketch lightly through the natural creases in pale brown.

OUNDS

If you have ever wondered how they create those gory scenes on television, here's how. With the help of special makeup, you can produce a fake wound that will fool your family and friends into rushing for the bandages. Follow the instructions below to create a gruesome knife slash and then use the same techniques to create bullet holes, bruises and other wounds.

The products you will need to create special effects are:

Derma wax

Translucent powder

Cold cream

Film blood (or fake blood capsules from toy or theatrical suppliers)

Water-based paint

Spatula

Stipple sponge

Coffee grounds

Orange stick

KNIFE SLASH

1 Soften the wax in the tub by scraping the surface with the rounded end of a spatula. Build up a bump on the cheek by pressing small amounts of wax onto the skin with the spatula. Dab on a little cold cream and use your fingertips to smooth out the edges of the wax.

2 With an orange stick, or the end of a brush, cut a crevice into the wax. Be careful at this point not to get too close to the underlying skin. Mold and shape the open wound using cold cream and dust lightly with translucent powder.

3 Next use a stipple sponge and lightly apply some red paint to the outside edges to create the effect of bruising. Inside the wound opening, paint the bottom black for depth and red around the edges.

4 Pour some liquid film blood into a lid and add a few coffee grounds. Mix together lightly. Pick up these blood clots on a fine brush and position inside the wound. Finally apply some more of this liquid and let it run down the cheeks for a really gory effect!

BULLET WOUND

Using the same techniques you used for the knife slash, you can create a realistic bullet hole wound. The effect is even more dramatic if you add blood clots.

INDEX